For Monica
May all your highways
be thighways!
Happy Cooking!
Sara

Southern Thighways

Thigh Recipes With A Southern Accent

Sara T. Gibbs
and Tom Gibbs

Sara T. Gibbs

Border Springs Press
Louisville, Kentucky

ISBN 0-9769199-0-7

Published by Border Springs Press
P.O. Box 991425
Louisville, KY 40269-1425

Printed in Canada

Designed by Wm. Knox Gunn
set in Tom's New Roman by Tom Murphy fonts.tom7.com
and Summertime by Sara www.saraarts.com.

This book is dedicated to thigh-lovers everywhere

Thigh Way of Thinking

It might be just a little too risqué
To talk about thighs in any other way,
So I'll confine my humble musings
To those of chickens and culinary usings.

Nevertheless, there's no way I can deny
The best part of any leg is the thigh.
Although on chickens, they're often overlooked,
They serve up quite tasty any way they're cooked.

Give cattle and catch some needed relief,
Use thigh meat in place of seafood or beef.
Soups and stews will be just as hearty.
Feature thighs as entrée at a dinner party.

Enter the mystery of the way of the thigh:
Whether you soup, stew, grill, braise, smoke, or fry,
The meal that goes to table will be haute cuisine
So pardon the diners who lick their platters clean.

Contents

Sundown Suppers

Acknowledgments

Now that the hard part is done, it's time to tackle the difficult. How do I thank, sufficiently, the many people who helped get this project from idea to test kitchen to finished book? The best way, I think, is to just offer a simple, straight forward, but gracious, thank you to all those folks—and put their names in print for whatever modicum of glory and posterity that may afford them. So, Thank you...

To my husband, Tom, who helped considerably with the writing and editing of the book but, also, as cook's assistant and dishwasher (with the help of Shorty the Cat) and as my constant cheerleader.

To Darlene Webb for the charming illustrations and to Jessie Kriech for her patience during our photography sessions.

To Sally Kraus, John Uhl, and Debbie Hunt who participated as both independent recipe testers and tasters and, too, their families, who also took part in (endured?) the tasting.

To my unflagging tasters, Brenda and Jerry Hancock, Joyce and Moe Miller, and the staff at Lynn's Paradise Café.

To my mother, Mabel Lyons Thompson, Sarah Fritschner, John T. Edge, and Bill Butler who all served me well as advisers throughout the entire process of making this book a reality.

To Lynn Winter and Lori Pritchett who offered encouragement and support from beginning to end.

Again, Thank you all.

Introduction

Every meal is a kind of journey and so is every recipe. Whether sitting down to a fine meal prepared by someone else or preparing the food ourselves, we take a sort of journey that is often through both time and space. Every aroma, every taste, allows us to travel, if only for a instant, and if only unconsciously, to places where certain ingredients or dishes first originated, and to times when we first tasted them. Meals can also be a journey into our own lives; the times and places we come from and, maybe, the times and places we are going—with family or friends.

Friends are certainly an essential part of life, but when it comes right down to it, home-cooking is home-cooking, with its strongest roots in family. Our earliest memories of eating are of meals our mothers, and maybe sometimes our fathers, cooked for us when we were growing up. And if Grandma and Grandpa didn't cook for us directly, they surely passed along what they knew to our mommas and daddies. Not that long ago, twenty or thirty years at most, the whole family ate together and meals were often the family media outlets. The kitchen table was where we caught up on what each other was doing in the world outside the home. That time around that table is where so many of our fondest memories come from.

My own journeys with food began in Western Maryland, where I grew up, just south of the Mason-Dixon Line, on the border with West Virginia. Early on, I ventured out into new and exciting places and dishes when my family began taking summer trips to the North Carolina coast and winter trips to Florida. In all of our travels, my parents always preferred the homey local cafes and restaurants with their meat-and-three meals made fresh with fresh ingredients. Naturally, as we traveled farther South and closer to the coast, I discovered exciting new dishes and their flavors, many of which have stayed with me to this day. That's what Southern Thighways is all about—journeys, and making memories.

The book takes a culinary journey into the South and, hopefully, into the homes, hearts, and hungry bellies of families and friends throughout the country. All the recipes are written so that they can be prepared by the solo cook, who will be able to sit back and reap the accolades, or orchestrated to include the whole family or a group of friends in the preparation so that everyone finishes the journey to mutual culinary cheers. (On that note, I might remind of Henny Penny and her bread plans, but that might be in poor taste since she'll be in the pot soon enough—at least her thighs will.)

You might well ask, Why thighs? Good question. Thighs tend to be tender, juicy, and, likely, the most succulent part of the chicken. Thighs are delicious by themselves, and they readily take on, and are enhanced by, a multitude of other flavors. They make good eating with all but two cooking methods—under-cooking or over-cooking. In addition to all those fine reasons, the most honest answer to the question is that the thigh is my own favorite part of the chicken and I think, considering its versatility in cooking, it is too often neglected, especially these days, in favor of the ever-present boneless, skinless chicken breast which, quite frankly, is pretty boring.

So, come on along on this journey down Southern Thighways and discover new and exciting recipes which will yield some of the most unique, flavorful, and memorable dishes to tantalize your taste buds, as well as those of family and friends.

Day Starters and Light Meals

Chicken-for-Breakfast Strips

Green Chile Chicken Enchiladas

Fiesta Breakfast Casserole

Smokin' Thighs Cornbread Salad

Oven-Fried Chicken Salad with Apples & Asiago
    Mustard Vinaigrette

Cilantro Pecan Pesto Chicken Salad

Comfort Quesadillas with Southern Comfort
    Red Pepper Jelly Sauce

Barnyard and Bayou Quesadillas
    with Crayfish Salsa

Chicken Logic: Naturally

Go natural! Natural chicken is the best, and healthier, because it has no additives and, like homegrown vegetables, retains its "real" and, well, natural flavor. A lot of chicken in grocery stores these days has been injected with a sodium solution that makes the meat much saltier and leaves an almost chemical aftertaste in the final product.

Chicken-for-Breakfast Strips

A delicious (maybe even a little healthier) alternative to processed pork products that are traditionally served with breakfast.

1 pound boneless, skinless chicken thighs

For the marinade:
1 cup buttermilk
1 teaspoon salt
1 tablespoon grated onion

For the breading:
1 cup flour
2 tablespoons cornstarch
1 teaspoon ground sage
1 teaspoon poultry seasoning
1½ teaspoons paprika
1½ teaspoons salt
½ teaspoon freshly ground black pepper
2 dashes ground nutmeg
Vegetable oil for frying

Cook's Secret:

The seasonings added to the flour are similar to those used in breakfast sausage. For an even smokier breakfast flavor, substitute hickory smoked salt for regular salt.

Trim the chicken thighs of any visible excess fat. Place a sheet of plastic wrap on a cutting board. Lay one thigh flat on top and cover with another sheet of plastic wrap. Pound with a meat mallet until the chicken is ¼ inch thick. Set aside and repeat with remaining chicken. Cut the flattened chicken into 1-inch strips.

For the marinade: Stir the marinade ingredients together in a medium-sized bowl. Add the flattened chicken strips and stir until well moistened. Marinate for 15 minutes.

For the breading: While the chicken is marinating, whisk the breading ingredients together in another bowl. Set aside.

After the chicken has finished marinating, drain it well in a colander and place it back in the bowl.

Heat about ½ cup vegetable oil in a large skillet over medium-high heat. Dredge the chicken strips in the seasoned flour and fry in batches until dark golden brown and cooked through, about 2–3 minutes per side. Drain on paper towels and keep warm in a low oven until all the strips are cooked.

Serve with eggs, grits and biscuits with honey butter.

Serves 6

Green Chile Chicken Enchiladas

For the Chicken:

1¾ - 2 pounds chicken thighs, skin & excess fat removed
½ large onion
1 teaspoon ground cumin
2 cups water
1 (14½-ounce) can chicken broth (not low-sodium)

For the Green Chile Sauce:

2 tablespoons olive oil or bacon grease
½ teaspoon minced garlic
½ cup diced onion
3 tablespoons flour
3 cups chicken broth (from cooked chicken)
¼ teaspoon cayenne pepper
½ teaspoon ground cumin
½ teaspoon Mexican oregano (optional)
8 ounces fresh Anaheim green chile peppers, parched, peeled, seeded, and diced (see Cook's Secret) or 4½ ounces canned diced green chiles (mild)

For the Enchiladas:

12 (5-inch) corn tortillas
8 ounces Mexican blend shredded cheese
Pico de Gallo (see recipe)
4 fried eggs (optional)

For the Chicken: Place the chicken thighs, onion, cumin, water and chicken broth in a 5-quart Dutch oven and bring to a boil. Skim any foam that comes to the surface, then reduce the heat to a light simmer, cover and cook for 1 hour or until the meat pulls easily from the bones. Remove from the heat and strain, reserving the broth and the chicken. When cool enough to handle, remove the meat from the bones and chop. Set aside.

For the Green Chile Sauce: Wipe out the pan and return to medium-high heat. Add the olive oil or bacon grease, then stir in the onion and sauté for 2 – 3 minutes or until the onions begin to soften. Stir in the garlic and sauté until you can smell its aroma, about 30 seconds. Stir in the flour and cook for 30 seconds, then add the reserved chicken broth and remaining ingredients. Whisk thoroughly and bring to a boil, then reduce the heat and simmer for about 20 minutes or until the sauce has reduced and thickened.

Remove the pot from the heat and puree the sauce with a hand-held blender. Keep warm until ready to use.

For the Enchiladas: Soften the tortillas one at a time, by heating them on a warm cast-iron griddle or sauté pan. They should puff slightly, but not heat long enough to get crisp.

Place about ¼ cup of the chopped chicken in each tortilla and roll it up tightly. Place in an individual oven-proof baking dish. Continue with the remaining tortillas in assembly-line fashion until all the ingredients have been used. You should use three rolled tortillas for each casserole. Cover each casserole with 1/3 cup of Green Chile Sauce and ½ cup of cheese. Bake for 10 – 12 minutes or until the cheese melts and bubbles.

Top each with a fried egg (if using) and Pico de Gallo and serve immediately.

Serves 4

Variation:

Another variation is to prepare a full casserole using a 13 x 9 baking dish, rather than individual portions. It is a little messier to serve, but tastes just as good. Simply roll all of the tortillas and line them up in a well-greased 13 x 9 casserole, top with 1½ cups green chile sauce and cover with all of the cheese. It will take a little longer to bake, about 15 minutes or so. Top with the fried eggs (if using) and serve the Pico de Gallo on the side. The chicken and sauce can be prepared ahead of time and refrigerated, then assembled and baked as needed.

Cook's Secret:

To parch fresh green chile peppers, cut a 1-inch slit in each pepper for steam to escape, place the peppers under the broiler for about 15 minutes, turning every 5 minutes for even parching. Skin is ready when it becomes a deep golden-brown color and begins to blister. Remove peppers from the broiler and place them in a bowl, then cover with plastic wrap, let stand until peppers have cooled enough to handle, then peel skin off. Skin should peel easily at this point. Cut lengthwise, open and remove the stem and seeds, now you're ready to dice the peppers. Sure, this takes more time and effort, but the flavor of fresh, roasted peppers certainly enhances the dish.

Fiesta Breakfast Casserole

This Tex-Mex inspiration can be presented in individual portions or as a unique addition to a breakfast buffet—both methods are given here—and it offers another tasty way to use that Smokin' Thigh chicken you've got on hand.

1 (16-ounce) can refried beans
2 cups chopped Smokin' Thighs (see recipe)
8 ounces Mexican blend shredded cheese
½ cup sour cream
1 cup Pico de Gallo (see recipe)
1 pound bag corn tortilla chips

Preheat oven to 400° F.

Prepare four individual baking dishes with non-stick spray. Spread ½ cup of refried beans over the bottom of each dish, then cover with ½ cup chopped smoked chicken. Drizzle each with about a tablespoon of taco sauce, and then cover with ½ cup of shredded cheese. Bake for 10 – 12 minutes, or until cheese melts and bubbles around the edges.

While the dip is baking, scramble the eggs. When the cheese has melted and the dip has heated through, remove from the oven and top each casserole with some of the scrambled eggs, some sour cream and Pico de Gallo.

Serve immediately with tortilla chips on the side for dipping.

Serves 6

Buffet Variation:

Another variation is to prepare a full casserole using a 13x9 baking dish, rather than individual portions. Simply spread the entire can of beans on the bottom, drizzle with about ¼ cup taco sauce, sprinkle with 2 cups of smoked chicken and cover with all of the cheese. It will take a little longer to bake, about 15 minutes or so. Top with the eggs and garnishes and serve with the chips on the side.

Smokin' Thighs Cornbread Salad

A featured recipe in Southern Living magazine. Serve as either an appetizer, a light lunch on salad greens dressed with basil vinaigrette, or as a brunch entrée with poached eggs and fruit.

4 slices applewood smoked bacon
1 (6-ounce) package cornbread
1¼ cups mayonnaise
¼ cup minced Vidalia onions
2 tablespoons chiffonade of fresh basil
2 tablespoons lemon juice
¼ teaspoon coarse ground black pepper
1 cup cooked fresh lima beans or other fresh butter beans
1 cup cooked fresh corn kernels (from 2 ears of corn)
½ cup diced red bell pepper
2 cups shredded Smokin' Thighs (see recipe)
8 slices homegrown tomato
Garnish: chopped fresh chives

Cook's Secret:

This Southern version of panzanella (Italian bread salad) can provide a great way to use leftovers. Friday night's smoked chicken supper with corn on the cob and cornbread can easily become Saturday's brunch.

Dice bacon and fry until crisp in a 6½-inch cast iron skillet. Drain bacon on paper towels and set aside. Pour the bacon grease out of the pan, leaving just enough to coat the surface. Prepare the cornbread according to package directions. Pour into the cast iron skillet and bake until golden brown. Cool, then crumble or dice into a large bowl. Set aside.

Whisk the mayonnaise, Vidalia onions, basil, lemon juice and black pepper in a smaller bowl. Fold into crumbled cornbread along with lima beans, corn kernels, diced red bell pepper, smoked chicken and reserved chopped bacon. Mix until all ingredients are moistened.

Place a slice of tomato on each serving plate. Mound the cornbread salad on top and garnish with fresh chives.

Serves 8

Oven-Fried Chicken Salad
with Apples & Asiago

This is a healthier rendition of the ever-popular fried chicken salad. The chicken is oven-fried using olive oil and Panko bread crumbs.

1 pound boneless, skinless chicken thighs

For the marinade:
2 tablespoons creamy Dijon mustard
2 tablespoons dry white wine
1 teaspoon Creole seasoning
2 tablespoons olive oil

For the breading:
1½ cups Panko bread crumbs
1 teaspoon Creole seasoning
2 tablespoons olive oil

For the salad:
2 Gala apples
12 cups mixed salad greens
4 ounces Asiago cheese (or other aged white cheese), thinly sliced
1 cup toasted hazelnuts
Mustard Vinaigrette (see recipe)

Trim excess fat from thighs and place on a cutting board between two sheets of plastic wrap. Using a meat tenderizer, pound the chicken briefly until it is ¼-inch thick. Cut into ½-inch strips and set aside.

For the marinade: In a medium-sized bowl, whisk together the Dijon, dry white wine, Creole seasoning and olive oil. Add the chicken to the marinade and mix well. Marinate at room temperature for 15 minutes.

For the breading: Thoroughly mix the bread crumbs and Creole seasoning in a shallow bowl, then drizzle the olive oil over the crumbs and blend in with a rubber spatula. Set aside.

Preheat the oven to 450° F. Roll the chicken strips in the seasoned Panko breadcrumbs and place on a well-greased baking sheet. Bake for 15 - 20 minutes or until the chicken is crispy and the meat is opaque when cut with a knife.

For the salad: Core and thinly slice the apples, then place in a large bowl along with the salad greens and toss with the mustard vinaigrette. Divide the dressed greens among four dinner plates, then garnish with Asiago cheese, chicken strips and toasted hazelnuts.

Serves 4

> **Cook's Secret:**
> Panko bread crumbs are lighter, crispier, Japanese style bread crumbs that hold up well and stay crispy right through cooking to serving. If you don't have an Asian market near you, most grocery stores do carry panko—check the Asian foods section.

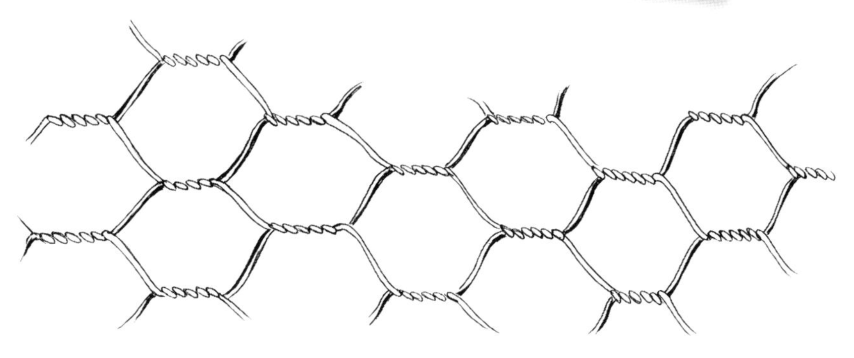

Mustard Vinaigrette

¼ cup cider vinegar
2 teaspoons brown sugar
1½ teaspoons Dijon mustard
½ teaspoon salt
Freshly ground black pepper to taste
¾ cup vegetable or salad oil

Place all ingredients in a small jar. Secure the lid tightly and shake well until blended.

Yield: About 1 cup

Cilantro Pecan Pesto Chicken Salad

This chicken salad is a tangy departure from sweet and fruity chicken salads and pairs well with homegrown tomatoes, cucumbers, and olives for a cool summer supper. It's also a fine topping for baby greens with a red wine vinaigrette.

2 cups diced poached chicken thighs (see recipe)
¾ cup diced celery
½ cup toasted chopped pecans
½ cup mayonnaise
2 teaspoons fresh lime juice
¼ cup Cilantro Pecan Pesto (see recipe)
Salt and freshly ground black pepper to taste

Place the diced chicken thighs, diced celery and pecans in a medium-sized bowl and toss to mix thoroughly. Set aside.

Whisk the mayonnaise, lime juice and ¼ cup pesto in a small bowl until well blended. Carefully fold the pesto mayonnaise into the chicken mixture. Taste and season with salt and pepper.

Chill for about 30 minutes prior to serving to allow the flavors to blend.

Serves 4

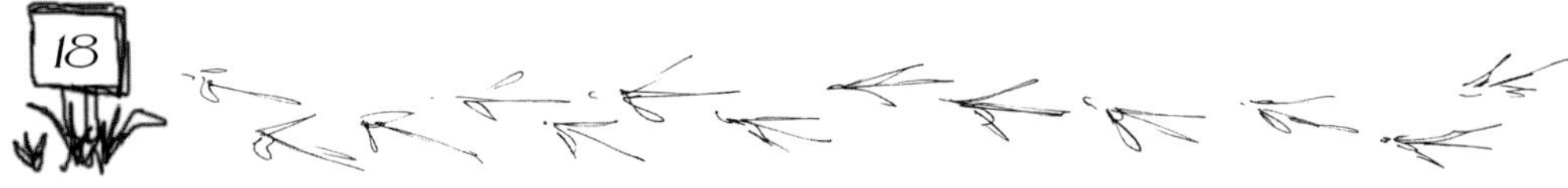

Cilantro Pecan Pesto

This pesto recipe yields more than the chicken salad requires; but don't worry, it's a great condiment to have on hand for a tasty addition to grilled cheese sandwiches and to shrimp & grilled onion quesadillas.

¾ cup olive oil
½ cup pecan pieces
¾ cup Parmesan cheese
½ teaspoon black pepper
½ teaspoon salt
2 garlic cloves, chopped
1 bunch cilantro, washed & picked free of stems (about 3 cups)
1 tablespoon fresh lime juice

Cook's Secret:

Toast those pecans! To toast the pecans, spread them on a baking sheet and bake in a 350° F oven for 5-10 minutes. This helps release the natural oils, enhancing the flavor.

Place olive oil, pecans, Parmesan cheese, black pepper, salt and garlic in food processor and pulse until a paste forms. Add cilantro while blade is running and process until smooth.

Blend in the lime juice and taste. Add more salt or other seasonings if necessary.

Refrigerate until ready for use.

Yield: 1¼ cups

Comfort Quesadillas

South of the Mason-Dixon meets south-of-the-border in a recipe that makes a fine entrée, appetizer, or snack. Remember to grill the Smokin' Thighs ahead of time.

1 tablespoon butter
1 tablespoon oil
1 large sweet onion, cut in thin strips
2 cups diced Smokin' Thighs (see recipe)
4 slices cooked crisp bacon, crumbled
¼ cup coarsely chopped cilantro
1 cup shredded Monterey Jack cheese
1 cup crumbled feta cheese
8 (7-inch) flour tortillas
Southern Comfort Pepper Jelly Sauce (see recipe)

Heat butter and oil in large sauté pan over medium-high heat, then add onions and cook, stirring often until they begin to brown. Reduce the heat and cook until onions have caramelized to a golden brown. Remove from heat and stir in the chopped chicken, bacon and cilantro. Mix well.

Lay out one tortilla and spread ½ cup chicken mixture over bottom half, top with 2 tablespoons of each cheese, then fold the top half down to form a half moon. Repeat with remaining ingredients to form 8 quesadillas.

Grill quesadillas in a lightly oiled sauté pan over medium heat until golden brown and cheese has melted, about 2 minutes per side. Cut in wedges and serve with Southern Comfort Pepper Jelly Sauce (see recipe).

Serves 8 as an appetizer or 4 as a meal

Southern Comfort® Pepper Jelly Sauce

1 (10-ounce) jar red pepper jelly
2 tablespoons hoisin sauce
1 teaspoon Sriracha chili sauce
¼ cup Southern Comfort
1½ tablespoons cornstarch
¼ cup apple juice

Heat red pepper jelly, hoisin sauce, Sriracha and Southern Comfort in a small saucepan over medium-low heat, stirring occasionally until smooth and bubbly.

In a small cup, whisk together the cornstarch and apple juice to make a binder. Whisk the cornstarch mixture into the sauce and blend well. Simmer until thickened.

Cool to room temperature and set aside. Serve with Comfort Quesadillas (see recipe) or egg rolls.

Yield: 1¾ cups

Cook's Secret:

Southern Comfort was originally created in New Orleans and is classified as a liqueur. It makes a fine ingredient for cooking and adds a slightly sweet, spicy, citrus flavor.

Barnyard & Bayou Quesadillas

From the barnyard, we get the chicken and from the bayou, the crayfish. Using the recipe in this book, make a batch of Smokin' Thighs ahead of time—the meat holds well in the freezer on or off the bone.

For the Yellow Rice:
1 tablespoon butter
1 tablespoon olive oil
½ cup diced onion
1 cup long-grain rice
1 teaspoon turmeric
½ teaspoon coriander
½ teaspoon cumin
¼ teaspoon cayenne pepper
1 teaspoon salt
2 cups water

> **Cook's Secret:**
> The Yellow Rice recipe used here makes a fine side dish for a variety of entrees.

For the Quesadillas:
8 (7-inch) flour tortillas
8 ounces Mexican blend shredded cheese
½ cup diced red onion
2 cups diced Smokin' Thighs (see recipe)
Melted butter or vegetable oil
Crayfish Salsa (see recipe)

For the Yellow Rice: Heat butter and olive oil in a saucepan over medium high heat. Add the diced onion and sauté for about 2 minutes, then stir in the rice, coating it with the oil. Stir in the spices & salt and sauté briefly, then add the water. Bring to a boil, then reduce heat and simmer for 15–20 minutes or until rice is done. Remove from heat and set aside to cool.

For the Quesadillas: Place ¼ cup cheese on the lower half of each tortilla, top with 2 tablespoons of rice, ¼ cup of diced chicken and 1 tablespoon of diced red onion. Fold the top half down over the filling and press lightly to seal. Repeat with remaining tortillas.

Heat a cast iron griddle or sauté pan over medium heat. Brush the quesadillas with melted butter or vegetable oil and cook until golden brown and cheese has melted, about 3 minutes per side. Cut into wedges and serve with Crayfish Salsa (see recipe).

Serves 8 as an appetizer or 4 as a meal

Crayfish Salsa

1 (8-ounce) package frozen crayfish tail meat, thawed, drained and chopped
$^1/_3$ cup diced red bell pepper
2 tablespoons coarsely chopped cilantro
½ cup diced tomato
1 jalapeno pepper, seeded and minced
½ teaspoon minced garlic
1 teaspoon Kosher salt
1 tablespoon fresh lime juice

Mix all ingredients together in a small bowl and refrigerate for 30 minutes to allow the flavors to blend.

Yield: 2½ cups

Well, I Declare!

Watch out. Many of the crayfish sold today are imported from the Orient — while they may be adequate, they ain't Southern! Make the effort to find authentic, Southern born and bred crayfish.

Soups and Stews

Thighways Chicken Stock

Quick Poach 'n' Stock

Aunt Louise's Chicken Soup with Slipdowns

Chicken Shiitake Barley Soup

Bourbon Chicken Corn Chowder

South by SW Chicken Rice Soup

Chesapeake Bay Chicken Vegetable Soup

Low Country Chicken Soup

Brunswick Stew

Chicken and Sausage Gumbo

Notcher Traditional Chicken Stew

Chicken and Twice-a-Year Noodles

Chicken Logic: Takin' Stock

Sure, making your own chicken stock from scratch takes both time and effort but it is always well worth the task. Not only is the end result a better product all the way around—having a richer, more full-bodied flavor—but it also allows you to season to your own taste. Don't forget, it freezes just fine.

Thighways Chicken Stock

This is a traditional, long-cooking stock. Fat content can be reduced by refrigerating overnight to let the fat rise to the surface, making it easy to skim off and discard.

1 tablespoon butter
2 pounds chicken thighs
3 quarts cold water
1 cup diced yellow onion
1 carrot, chopped (about ½ cup)
1 rib of celery, chopped (about ½ cup)
3 black peppercorns or ½ teaspoon freshly ground pepper
½ teaspoon salt
A sprig of parsley
A sprig of thyme

Heat 1 tablespoon of butter in a 5-quart Dutch oven over medium heat. Add the thighs and cook until light golden, about 3 minutes per side. Do not allow the meat to brown. Add the cold water, increase the heat to medium-high and bring to a boil. Skim any foam that comes to the surface, then add the remaining ingredients and return to a boil.

Reduce and regulate the heat so that the mixture barely simmers and cook for 2 hours, stirring occasionally. The stock should reduce slightly.

Remove the meat and set aside, then strain the stock. Discard the vegetables, herbs and peppercorns.

Skin and bone the thighs and dice any usable meat. Store in refrigerator and use in recipes calling for poached chicken, although it will not have as much flavor as those cooked by the Poach 'n' Stock method

Refrigerate the stock overnight and before using remove any fat that has risen to the surface.

Yield: About 2 quarts

Quick Poach 'n' Stock

This recipe/technique yields both an adequate stock and poached chicken. Chicken stock normally takes 2-3 hours to prepare but this "quick method," while not as rich, improves the often metallic flavor of canned chicken broth by incorporating the natural flavors of chicken and fresh vegetables.

1 tablespoon butter
1 rib celery, chopped (about ½ cup)
1 cup chopped onion
1 carrot, chopped (about ½ cup)
1 sprig fresh thyme
1 sprig fresh parsley
Several grindings of black pepper
1 quart cold water
2 (14½-ounce) cans chicken broth (not low-sodium)
1¾ to 2 pounds bone-in chicken thighs, skin and excess fat removed

Heat butter in 5-quart stockpot over medium heat. Add celery, onion, carrots, and thyme and parsley. Sauté for about 2-3 minutes, or until vegetables begin to soften.

Add water, chicken broth and chicken thighs. Bring to a boil. Skim any foam that accumulates on the surface of the liquid. Reduce the heat and simmer for 20 minutes.

Remove from the heat, cover and allow the mixture to steep for 30 minutes.

Lift out the chicken thighs and set aside to cool. When cool enough to handle, remove the meat from the bones. Trim any excess fat and discard along with bones. Chop or shred the meat for use in soups, salads or stews.

Strain the stock and refrigerate overnight or use immediately in any recipe. When ready to use, remove any hardened fat that has risen to the surface.

Yield: 2 quarts

A piece of friendly advice:

Refrigerating overnight makes it easy to skim any remaining fat from the top of the stock, but is not absolutely necessary since removing the skin before cooking reduces the fat content considerably.

Aunt Louise's Chicken Soup with Slipdowns

My great-aunt Louise called these tender little dumplings "slipdowns" because they slip easily into the broth and they slide down easy with the eating. The Amish call the dumplings "rivels." In late summer, a cup of fresh sweet white corn makes a delicious addition to the soup.

For the soup:
2 quarts homemade chicken broth or low-sodium chicken broth
2 cups diced poached chicken thighs (see recipe)
1 cup diced yellow onions
½ cup diced carrots
½ cup diced celery
¼ teaspoon poultry seasoning

For the slipdowns:
1 egg, beaten
2 tablespoons Parmesan cheese
2 teaspoons minced fresh parsley
¼ cup cold water
¼ teaspoon salt
Three grindings of black pepper
½ cup plus 2 tablespoons all-purpose flour

Cook's Secret:
Hate to cut vegetables? Most grocery store produce departments carry carrots and celery already cut into sticks for easier dicing.

For the soup: Place all the ingredients for the soup in a 5-quart Dutch oven and bring to a boil over medium-high heat. Reduce the heat, cover and simmer for 30 minutes or until vegetables are tender.

For the slipdowns: While the soup is cooking, prepare the slipdowns. Whisk the egg, Parmesan cheese, parsley, water, salt and pepper in a medium-sized bowl until smooth. Sift the flour over the batter and mix well. Let the mixture sit at room temperature for at least 30 minutes.

When the vegetables are tender, regulate the heat so that the soup maintains a light simmer. Tilt the bowl over the broth so that the batter begins to drip over the edge. Cut the batter into narrow strips with a large metal spoon and allow them to drop into the simmering broth. Continue until you have used about ⅓ of the batter, then stop and stir the soup carefully. The dumplings should hold together in irregular shapes. Repeat until you have used all the batter, stirring occasionally.

When all of the batter has been used, cover the soup and simmer for another 3 minutes to make sure the slipdowns have cooked through. Serve immediately.

Yield: 2½ quarts

Chicken Shiitake Barley Soup

Traditionally made with beef, thigh meat offers a unique change-of-pace.

1 tablespoon olive oil
2 cups diced onion
1 cup diced celery
1 cup diced carrots
½ teaspoon minced garlic
2 quarts homemade chicken stock or low-sodium chicken broth
1 (8-ounce) can Italian-seasoned tomato sauce
¼ cup merlot or other fruity red wine
7 ounces shiitake mushrooms, stemmed & cut into thin strips
2 cups diced poached chicken thighs (see recipe)
1 cup quick barley, cooked according to packaged directions, drained & well-rinsed
2 tablespoons minced fresh basil
Salt & freshly ground pepper to taste
Garnish: Minced fresh parsley

Heat olive oil in a 5-quart stockpot over medium heat. Add onion, celery, carrots and garlic and sauté for 2 minutes, or until the vegetables begin to soften.

Add chicken stock, tomato sauce, merlot, mushrooms & diced chicken and bring to a boil. Reduce the heat and simmer for 30 minutes or until vegetables are tender.

Stir in the cooked and rinsed barley and fresh basil, then season with salt and freshly-ground black pepper. Return to a simmer and cook for another 10 minutes.

Garnish with minced fresh parsley.

Yields: 3 quarts

Cook's Secret:

Rinsing the barley removes some of the starch so the soup will not become heavy and gelatinous.

Well, I Declare!

Barley has been used as sustenance since the Stone Age. The ancient Sumerians even used it as money and ancient Greek athletes considered it more strengthening than other grains. In the South, it's a key ingredient in bourbon.

Bourbon Chicken Corn Chowder

Features three of the South's most beloved ingredients: Corn, bourbon, and bacon.

4 strips bacon, diced
1 cup diced fresh leeks
1½ cups diced yellow onion
1 cup diced celery
1 cup diced carrots
½ teaspoon minced garlic
Dash red pepper flakes
⅓ cup flour
2 quarts homemade or low-sodium chicken stock
3 small red potatoes, cubed (about 2 cups)
1 (1-lb.) bag frozen corn (or fresh corn kernels removed from 6 ears)
2 cups diced poached chicken thighs (see recipe)
2 cups fat-free half & half (or regular half & half)
2 tablespoons bourbon
Salt and freshly ground black pepper to taste
Garnish: Minced fresh parsley and reserved cooked bacon

Fry bacon over medium heat until crisp. Remove from the pan and set aside to drain on paper towels, leaving 2 tablespoons of bacon grease in the pan. Return the pan to medium high heat and add leeks, onions, celery, carrots, garlic, red pepper flakes and sauté for about 3 minutes or until vegetables begin to soften.

Sprinkle flour over the vegetables and sauté for another minute, stirring constantly. Add chicken stock, red potatoes, corn and diced chicken and bring to a boil. Reduce heat to a simmer and cook for 30 - 40 minutes or until vegetables are tender, stirring occasionally.

Remove from the heat. Whisk in the half & half and bourbon, then season with salt and freshly ground black pepper. Serve garnished with minced fresh parsley and reserved cooked bacon.

Yield: 3½ quarts

<u>A piece of friendly advice:</u> Always clean leeks thoroughly. To do this, cut off root tip and the dark green leaves. Cut the leeks lengthwise and rinse under cold, running water. After dicing, put leeks in a colander and rinse again under cold, running water. Remember to wash cutting board to remove sand and grit before reusing.

South by Southwest Chicken Rice Soup

This recipe brings together the great Southern staple, rice, with some of the staple ingredients of the American Southwest. This recipe was inspired by my many trips to my husband's home state of Texas and by our trips to New Mexico.

2 pounds chicken thighs, skin and excess fat removed
1 quart cold water
2 (14½-ounce) cans chicken broth (not low-sodium)
1 (10-ounce) can diced tomatoes and green chiles
½ cup diced onions
2 tablespoons chili powder
½ teaspoon ground cumin
½ cup raw long grain white rice,
cooked according to package directions
Pico de Gallo, for garnish (see recipe)

Place the chicken thighs, water, chicken broth, canned tomatoes & green chiles, diced onions, chili powder and cumin in a 5-quart Dutch oven and bring to a boil over medium-high heat. Reduce to a simmer, cover and simmer gently for 1 hour and 15 minutes, or until meat pulls easily away from the bone. Remove from the heat.

Using tongs, lift the chicken out of the broth and set aside to cool. When cool enough to handle, shred into small pieces and return to the broth. Bring the soup back to a simmer and cook for another 5 minutes, stirring often so that the chicken begins to shred and separate. Stir in the cooked rice and serve immediately, garnished with Pico de Gallo.

Yield: 2 quarts

Pico de Gallo

2 large jalapeno peppers,
seeded and minced
½ cup diced fresh tomato
½ cup diced sweet white onion
1 garlic clove, minced
2 tablespoons chopped fresh cilantro
Kosher salt to taste

Blend all ingredients together in small bowl. Cover and chill for at least one hour before serving.

Yield: 1¼ cups

South by Southwest Chicken Rice Soup

Chicken-for-Breakfast Strips

Oven-Fried Chicken Salad with Apples and Asiago

Cilantro Pecan Pesto Chicken Salad

Swanton Picnic Chicken

Sunshine State Stir-Fry

Maryland Fried Chicken

Chesapeake Bay Chicken Vegetable Soup

Chesapeake Bay Chicken Vegetable Soup

A "landlubber's" variation on the Crab-Vegetable soup long enjoyed all over Maryland. (A welcomed treat for those with shellfish allergies!)

> **Cook's Secret:**
> It's the Old Bay Seasoning that gives it that distinct "seafaring" flavor. Find it in the spice section of the grocery store or at the seafood counter.

1 tablespoon olive oil
2 cups diced yellow onions
2 carrots, cut lengthwise, then into thin slices or half moons (about 1 cup)
1 cup diced celery
8 ounces trimmed fresh green beans, cut in 1-inch pieces (about 1½ cups)
1¾ - 2 pounds chicken thighs, skin and excess fat removed
8 ounces Yukon Gold potatoes, in ½-inch cubes (about 1¾ cups)
1½ cups fresh or frozen yellow corn kernels
1 cup fresh or frozen baby lima beans
2 tablespoons Worcestershire sauce
1½ tablespoons Old Bay Seafood Seasoning
1 bay leaf
2 quarts homemade chicken stock or low-sodium chicken broth, divided
1 (28-ounce) can whole tomatoes

Heat the olive oil in an 8-quart heavy stock pot over medium high heat. Stir in the onions, carrots, celery and green beans and sauté for 2 - 3 minutes or until the vegetables begin to soften.

Add the chicken thighs, potatoes, corn, lima beans, Worcestershire sauce, Old Bay, bay leaf and 2 quarts homemade stock to the sautéed vegetable mixture. Using your hands, carefully squeeze the whole tomatoes and break into small pieces. Add to the pot, stir well and bring to a boil.

Reduce heat and simmer for 45 minutes, stirring occasionally.

Remove the chicken thighs and set aside to cool, and continue to simmer for another 30 minutes. When the chicken is cool, remove it from the bones, then chop the meat and stir it into the soup. Remove the bay leaf and taste for seasoning.

Serve with chowder crackers.

Yield: 1 gallon

Low Country Chicken Soup

Very much like the famous Carolina She-crab soup but a delicious alternative—especially for the shellfish sensitive.

> **Cook's Secret:**
> The versatility of the hand-held blender allows the cook to puree right there in the soup pot without messy sloshing back and forth between pot and food processor or mixing bowl.

3 tablespoons butter
½ cup diced celery
½ cup diced onions
½ cup diced carrots
1 shallot, minced
¼ cup all-purpose flour
1 quart homemade or low-sodium chicken stock
1 teaspoon Old Bay Seasoning
1 teaspoon Worcestershire sauce
¼ teaspoon mace
1 cup heavy whipping cream
2 cups diced poached chicken thighs (see recipe)
2 tablespoons sherry
1 tablespoon fresh chopped parsley
Salt and freshly ground black pepper
Garnish: Minced hard-boiled eggs

Melt butter in 5-quart Dutch oven over medium heat. Stir in celery, onions, carrots, and shallots. Sauté for 3 minutes, then reduce heat to medium-low, cover and cook for 5 minutes, stirring occasionally, until softened.

Stir in the flour and cook for 1 minute. Whisk in the chicken broth, Old Bay Seasoning, Worcestershire sauce, mace and cream. Bring to a boil, then reduce heat and simmer for 15 minutes, stirring occasionally, until vegetables are very soft.

Remove the soup from the heat. Using a hand-held blender, puree the soup until it is somewhat smooth, but vegetables are still visible. Stir in the chicken and sherry and reheat just until the soup begins to steam. Taste and season with salt and freshly ground black pepper. Whisk in the fresh parsley and serve over a tablespoon of minced egg placed in the bottom of each cup or bowl.

Yield: 2 quarts

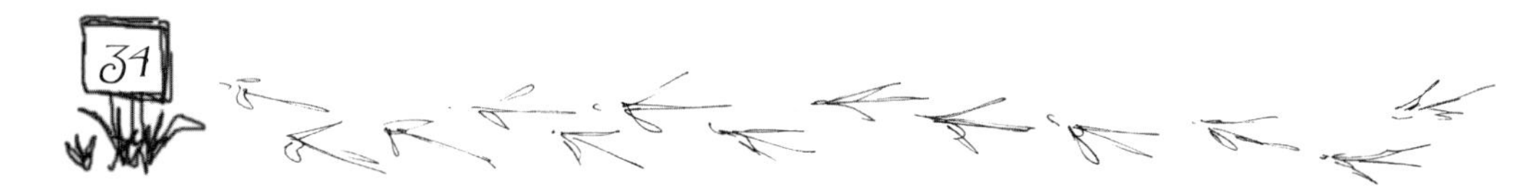

Brunswick Stew

This recipe takes two days to complete—you have to make the stock a day ahead—but will be well worth the time and effort once family and friends taste this delicious, albeit "controversial," stew (see below). It holds fine in the freezer, too.

3 pounds chicken thighs
3 pounds bone-in pork ribs
3 stalks celery, cut in half
2 carrots, scrubbed and cut in half
½ onion, peeled and cut in half
1 quart chicken broth
2 quarts water
3 cups baby lima beans
3 cups corn kernels
1 large onion (preferably a Vidalia), peeled and diced (about 3 cups)
2 (16-ounce) cans whole tomatoes—crushed by hand
1 pound Yukon Gold potatoes, peeled and diced (about 2½ cups)
1½ tablespoons Worcestershire sauce
2 tablespoons Louisiana-style hot sauce, divided
½ cup ketchup
1 tablespoon brown sugar
Salt and freshly ground black pepper

Well, I Declare!

The battle rages on! Georgia, Virginia, and North Carolina all lay claim to being the originator of Brunswick Stew and, to spice things up a bit, some claim the stew was first made by Native Americans who later taught it to the colonists.

Place chicken thighs, pork ribs, celery, carrots, onion, chicken broth and water in an 8-quart stock pot. Bring to a boil and skim off any foam that forms on the surface. Reduce to a simmer, cover and cook for 1½ hours or until the meat pulls easily from the bones. Remove the meat and set aside until cool enough to handle, then skin and bone, chopping all usable meat for the stew. Refrigerate until ready for use.

Strain the broth and refrigerate overnight so you can remove the fat that forms on the surface. You should have at least 3 quarts of stock.

Place the stock, lima beans, corn, diced onion, tomatoes, diced potatoes, Worcestershire sauce, 1 tablespoon hot sauce, ketchup, and brown sugar in an 8-quart stock pot and bring to a boil. Reduce heat and simmer for 1 hour. Stir in the diced meat, the remaining tablespoon hot sauce, season with salt and pepper and return to a simmer for another hour.

Yield: 5 quarts

Chicken & Sausage Gumbo

Using a smaller amount of roux than many recipes of its kind, the addition of okra helps thicken this one just right. The special method for preparing the roux is quicker and requires less time standing at the stove.

For the Roux:
1/3 cup all-purpose flour
3 tablespoons vegetable oil
For the Gumbo:
1 tablespoon vegetable oil
2 cups diced onion
1 cup diced celery
1 cup diced green bell pepper, (1 large)
1 tablespoon minced garlic
1 teaspoon minced fresh thyme
2 teaspoons Creole seasoning
¼ teaspoon cayenne pepper (or more to taste)
1½ quarts homemade chicken broth or
3 (14½-ounce) cans low-sodium chicken broth
1 (14½-ounce) can diced tomatoes
8 ounces cooked andouille sausage,
sliced lengthwise and then into ½-inch half moons
2 cups diced poached chicken thighs (see recipe)
10 ounces frozen or fresh diced okra
For garnish: sliced green onions and minced parsley
Cooked white rice

For the roux: Preheat oven to 350° F. Spread flour on baking sheet and bake for 45 minutes, stirring every 15 minutes. It should turn beige. Remove from oven and sift into a small bowl. Set aside. **NOTE:** You can bake a couple of cups at a time to keep on hand and use as needed.

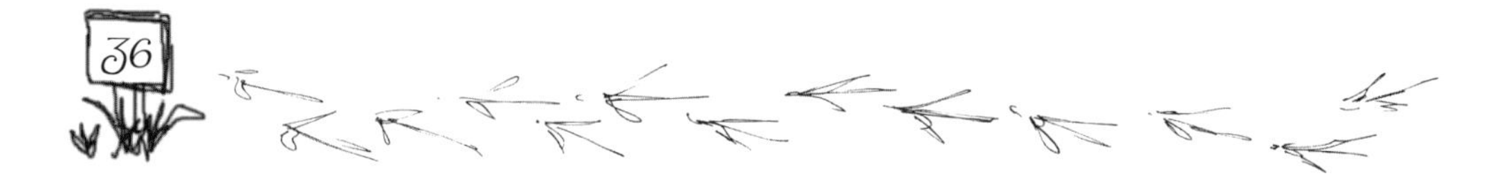

For the gumbo: Heat 3 tablespoons vegetable oil in a heavy 8-inch sauté pan over medium-heat. Whisk in the sifted baked flour. Cook for about 1½ minutes, stirring often. The roux should be the color of caramel. Set aside to cool.

Heat 1 tablespoon vegetable oil in a 5-quart Dutch oven over medium-high heat. Add onions, celery, green pepper, garlic, fresh thyme, Creole seasoning and cayenne pepper and sauté for 3 minutes. Add chicken stock, diced tomatoes, andouille sausage and diced chicken thighs. Bring to a boil, then whisk in the roux. Reduce to a simmer and cook for 30 minutes.

Add the okra and continue to simmer for another 15 minutes.

Season to taste with salt and pepper and serve over white rice garnished with green onions and minced parsley.

Yield: 10 cups

Notcher Traditional Chicken Stew

The mushrooms, fresh herbs, wine, and tomato sauce give this Southern stew a Mediterranean flavor.

2 tablespoons olive oil, divided
3 medium-size carrots, cut lengthwise then into ½-inch slices
3 ribs celery, cut lengthwise, then into ½-inch slices
2 cups diced yellow onion (¾-inch dice)
8 ounces fresh crimini mushrooms, halved or quartered if large
2 teaspoons minced fresh rosemary, divided
Salt and freshly ground black pepper
1¾ pound boneless, skinless chicken thighs, trimmed of excess fat and cut into ½-inch pieces
½ teaspoon minced fresh garlic
½ cup Merlot or other fruity red wine
½ cup tomato sauce
2 teaspoons Worcestershire sauce
2 cups low-sodium chicken stock
2 tablespoons minced fresh basil, divided
1 tablespoon cornstarch
Mashed potatoes
Minced fresh parsley, for garnish

Heat 1 tablespoon olive oil in a 5-quart Dutch oven over medium-high heat. Stir in the carrots, celery, onions, mushrooms and 1 teaspoon fresh rosemary. Season lightly with salt and freshly ground black pepper and sauté for 4 - 5 minutes or until beginning to brown. Pour the sautéed vegetables out into a large bowl and set aside.

Return the pan to medium-high heat and pour in the remaining tablespoon of olive oil. Add the diced chicken thighs, the remaining 1 teaspoon rosemary, and minced garlic, season lightly with salt and pepper and sauté for about 6 minutes or until opaque.

Deglaze with red wine, scraping any browned bits from the bottom of the pan. Stir the reserved sautéed vegetables back into the pan along with tomato sauce, Worcestershire sauce, chicken broth and fresh basil. Bring to a boil, then reduce heat, cover and simmer for 30 minutes.

Uncover and simmer for another 10 minutes to allow the stew to reduce. Whisk cornstarch into 1 tablespoon cold water and stir into the stew along with the remaining tablespoon of fresh basil. Simmer for 2 –3 minutes or until slightly thickened.

Serve over buttermilk mashed potatoes, garnished with fresh parsley.

Yield: 8 cups or 6 servings

Well, I Declare!

There's no taters in this stew! Nope, you serve this stew over creamy buttermilk mashed potatoes. Just another way to buck tradition a little.

Chicken and Twice-a-Year Noodles

Here's another one-dish meal that needs only the addition of a salad and bread. For folks who don't care for the soft texture of dumplings, these noodles are firmer and still have that hand-rolled appeal.

For the chicken:

1¾ -2 pounds bone-in chicken thighs, skin and excess fat removed

1 quart cold water

2 (14½-ounce) cans chicken broth

¾ cup diced onion

¼ cup diced celery

½ teaspoon salt

Several grindings of freshly ground black pepper

For the noodles:

2 tablespoons milk

2 eggs

1⅓ cups flour

1 teaspoon baking powder

1 teaspoon salt

For the chicken: Place the chicken thighs, water, chicken broth, diced onion, celery, salt and black pepper in a 5-quart Dutch oven and bring to a boil. Skim any foam that comes to the surface, then reduce to a simmer, cover and cook for 1 hour or until the meat pulls easily from the bone. Remove the chicken and set aside until cool enough to handle, then cut or shred into bite-sized pieces.

For the noodles: While the chicken is cooking, whisk the milk and eggs together until light and frothy in a small bowl, then sift in the flour, baking powder and salt. Work the flour mixture in with a rubber spatula until moistened, then turn out onto a floured surface and knead briefly to bring it together into a smooth dough.

Roll out as thin as possible (⅛-inch or less – you should get a circle 15 or 16 inches in diameter) on a floured surface and cut into strips, ½-inch by 5 inches, using a pizza cutter. Let the noodles rest while the chicken is cooking.

After removing the chicken, bring the broth to a boil and add the noodles carefully, stirring to prevent them from sticking. Reduce the heat to a simmer and cook for 15 - 20 minutes, stirring occasionally, until the noodles are almost tender. Add the chicken pieces and cook for another 5 minutes. Taste and add salt and pepper if necessary.

Serve in bowls with rolls and a green salad.

Serves 4 - 6

Cook's Secret:

I call these twice-a-year noodles because my mother has always prepared and served them in boullion for Thanksgiving and Christmas. Adding the thigh meat, to create a hearty one-dish supper, makes it well worth making the noodles from scratch. You can make the noodles the night before and let them dry on wax paper.

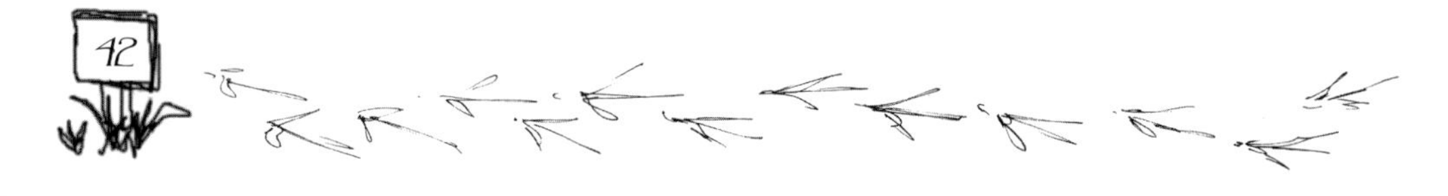

Sundown Suppers

Smokin' Thighs

Thighs in Cider Mushroom Gravy

Swanton Picnic Chicken

Purple Hull Peas and Rice

Cheerwine Barbecued Chicken

General Lee Chicken on
Cast Iron Green Tomato Fried Rice

Gulf Coast Bake

Scarlet Rice with Chicken

Sunshine State Stir Fry

Maryland Fried Chicken

Braised Chicken Thighs
with Bluegrass Summer
Succotash

Chicken Logic: Broth

I like to use low sodium canned chicken broth because of the health issue: but also because salt is something you can always add but you can never take away, once it's in there.

Smokin' Thighs

Smoke is as Southern as grits—and thighs love the smoke. For flavor variety, fiddle with the marinade ingredients. Try lime juice, vinegar, or wine. Try your own favorite herbs. Try minced shallots.

4 bone-in chicken thighs (about 1¾-2 pounds)
1 tablespoon olive oil
1 tablespoon lemon juice
½ teaspoon minced garlic
1 tablespoon chopped fresh basil
¼ teaspoon salt
1 cup hickory or pecan wood chips

Place chicken thighs in a shallow glass container. Whisk olive oil, lemon juice, minced garlic, basil and salt until well combined and pour over the chicken, turning to coat both sides. Cover and marinate at room temperature for one hour.

Soak wood chips in water for ½ an hour.

Light charcoal fire in bottom of covered grill. Allow to burn down for 15 – 20 minutes or until coals are red in the center and gray on the outside.

Drain wood chips thoroughly and scatter over the top of the coals.

Lift chicken from the marinade and drain slightly, then place thighs on food rack that has been prepared with non-stick spray.

Grill chicken, covered with grill lid, over medium-high heat (350° F to 400° F) 30 - 40 minutes or until done, turning occasionally.

Remove from grill and eat as is or cool until easy to handle, then remove skin and bones and chop the meat into bite-size pieces and refrigerate or freeze until ready for use in any recipe.

A piece of friendly advice:

Removing the skin after cooking reduces fat content. But if you must do that, be sure to brush the marinade under the skin, too, before letting the thighs marinate for the hour.

Thighs in Cider Mushroom Gravy

This dish is especially nice for Fall, when fresh cider becomes available. And be sure to use genuine pressed cider, not apple juice which is made from concentrate and doesn't have the same rich, earthy flavors that combine so well with the mushrooms.

⅓ cup flour
1 teaspoon salt
1 teaspoon paprika
1 teaspoon freshly ground black pepper
¼ cup vegetable oil
8 bone-in chicken thighs, (about 3½ - 4 pounds), skin & excess fat removed
1 tablespoon butter
8 ounces sliced button mushrooms
2 tablespoons minced shallots (about 1 large shallot)
½ teaspoon minced garlic
1 cup apple cider
2 cups low-sodium chicken broth or homemade chicken stock
1½ teaspoons dried tarragon
1 teaspoon Worcestershire sauce
½ cup heavy cream
Salt and freshly ground black pepper to taste
Cooked white rice or mashed potatoes
Garnish: Minced fresh parsley

Mix flour, salt, paprika and black pepper in shallow bowl. Heat a 12-inch non-stick skillet over medium-high heat. Pour in ¼ cup vegetable oil and heat until a sprinkle of flour sizzles on the surface.

Dredge the chicken thighs in the seasoned flour and add to the hot oil. You will have to do this in two batches to avoid overcrowding the pan. Brown the thighs until golden brown, about 3 –4 minutes per side. Remove the chicken and drain on paper towels.

Pour out the excess oil and wipe the pan clean with paper towels. Return the pan to medium heat and add 1 tablespoon of

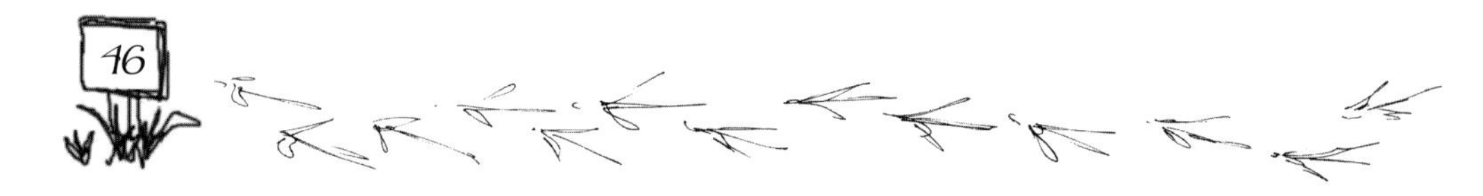

butter. When melted, stir in the mushrooms, shallots and garlic and sauté for 2 minutes or until soft. Whisk in the apple cider, chicken broth, tarragon and Worcestershire sauce.

Return the browned thighs to the pan and bring the mixture to a boil. Reduce the heat, cover and simmer for 30 minutes, turning once. Remove the chicken and set aside to keep warm. Whisk the cream into the sauce. Simmer until slightly thickened, about 5 minutes. Season to taste with salt and freshly ground black pepper.

Pile rice or mashed potatoes in shallow bowls. Place two thighs in each bowl and cover with the cider mushroom gravy. Garnish with fresh parsley.

Serves 4

Well, I Declare!

Virginia is noted for its apple production going all the way back to Thomas Jefferson, who called the mysterious Taliaferro variety that he grew the "best cyder apple existing." Why mysterious? Because since being grown at Monticello, the variety has disappeared completely from cultivation.

Swanton Picnic Chicken

This reminds me of chicken served at community picnics in Swanton, Maryland in the late 50's and early 60's. This is my own version of the carefully-guarded secret recipe that's still used today.

2 tablespoons butter
2 tablespoons olive oil
¼ cup fresh lemon juice
2 teaspoons Louisiana-style hot sauce
1 teaspoon garlic salt
1 teaspoon Worcestershire sauce
1 teaspoon paprika
1 teaspoon freshly ground black pepper
1 teaspoon Yucateco or other Mexican hot sauce
8 bone-in chicken thighs (3½ - 4 pounds)

Melt butter in a glass bowl in a microwave on 50% power. Whisk in remaining ingredients.

Place chicken thighs in a shallow glass container. Brush the marinade on both sides and under the skin. Cover and marinate at room temperature for one hour.

Light a charcoal fire in the bottom of a covered grill. Allow to burn down for 15 – 20 minutes or until coals are red in the center and gray on the outside.

Place thighs on food rack that has been prepared with non-stick spray.

Grill chicken, covered with grill lid, over medium-high heat (350° F to 400° F) 30 - 40 minutes or until done, turning occasionally.

Remove from the grill and serve immediately.

Serves 4

Cook's Secret:
The list of ingredients suggests a hot & spicy marinade but, after roasting or grilling, the flavor is lemony & slightly sharp without being HOT!

Note: This recipe can also be prepared in a tabletop rotisserie. Marinate the thighs as indicated above, then roast in the rotisserie, using a basket, for 45 minutes to one hour, depending on the size of the thighs.

Purple Hull Peas & Rice

A variation on the more traditional red beans & rice, the use of the smoked chicken makes for a healthier alternative to sausage and if you have the smoked chicken on hand already (see Smokin' Thighs recipe), this becomes a quick and easy weeknight supper.

1 tablespoon olive oil
1 cup diced yellow onion
1 cup diced green bell pepper
1 cup diced chopped celery
1 teaspoon minced garlic
2 teaspoons Creole seasoning
¼ teaspoon cayenne pepper (optional)
1 teaspoon minced fresh thyme
2 bay leaves
1½ quarts homemade or low-sodium chicken broth
2 cups diced Smokin' Thighs (see recipe)
3 (15½ -ounce) cans purple hull peas, drained and rinsed
Steamed long-grain white rice

Heat oil in a 5-quart Dutch oven over medium-high heat. Add onions, peppers, celery, garlic, Creole seasoning, cayenne (if using) and fresh thyme and sauté for 4 minutes, until vegetables begin to soften. Add bay leaves, chicken broth, and diced, smoked thighs, and bring to a boil, then reduce to a simmer and cook for 30 minutes, or until the vegetables are tender.

Stir in the purple hull peas and return to a simmer, then cook for another 15 minutes. Taste and season with salt and pepper, if necessary. Discard bay leaves.

Serve over white rice in shallow bowls.

Serves 6 - 8

Cook's Secret:

Using canned purple hull peas, reduces cooking time and gets this tasty supper to the table quicker. If you can't find purple hull peas, substitute black-eyed peas or crowder peas (so named because they are crowded together in the pod).

Cheerwine® Barbecued Chicken

Cheerwine is the delicious cherry-flavored soft drink that has been produced in Salisbury, North Carolina since 1917. It's unique taste makes for a refreshing cold beverage and the anchor of an exciting barbecue sauce.

Cheerwine Barbecue Sauce

1 tablespoon butter
½ teaspoon minced garlic
1 cup ketchup
1 cup Cheerwine
3 tablespoons Worcestershire sauce
¼ cup A-1 sauce
¼ teaspoon cayenne pepper
½ teaspoon black pepper
½ teaspoon dry mustard
2 tablespoons white distilled vinegar

Cook's Secret:

Can't find Cheerwine in your local grocery or specialty foods store? Don't despair, you can order it online from www.cheerwine.com.

Melt butter in a 2-quart heavy-bottomed saucepan over medium heat. Add the minced onion and sauté for 1 – 2 minutes, or until beginning to soften. Whisk in the remaining ingredients and mix well.

Bring the sauce to a boil, then reduce the heat to medium-low and simmer for 20 minutes. The sauce should be slightly thickened.

Cool, refrigerate and use as needed.

Yield: 2½ cups

For Rotisserie Barbecued Thighs:

Prepare the thighs and above. Spray a rotisserie basket with non-stick spray and secure thighs tightly in the basket. Cook for 1 hour or until a meat thermometer registers 170° F.

For Grilled Barbecued Thighs:

Light charcoal fire in bottom of covered grill. Allow to burn down for 15 – 20 minutes or until coals are red in the center and gray on the outside.

Place thighs on a food rack that has been prepared with non-stick spray.

Grill chicken, covered with grill lid, over medium-high heat (350° F to 400° F) 15 minutes, turning occasionally. Brush with Cheerwine Barbecue Sauce and grill for another 15 – 20 minutes, basting with more sauce as needed. Cook until a meat thermometer registers 170° F or until the juices run clear.

General Lee Chicken
on Cast Iron Green Tomato Fried Rice

A Southern spin on the Chinese dish, General Tso. The red pepper jelly and pecans give it that special Southern touch. Steamed green beans, stir-fried in sesame oil and a little garlic are a delicious accompaniment to this sweet, spicy stir-fry.

1¾ - 2 lb. Boneless, skinless chicken thighs, trimmed of excess fat
1 tablespoon Southern Comfort
1 tablespoon soy sauce
1 teaspoon cornstarch
3 tablespoons vegetable oil, divided
Red Pepper Jelly Sauce (see recipe)

For the Green Tomato Fried Rice:
3 slices applewood smoked bacon, cooked crisp and chopped
1 cup diced green tomatoes
¼ cup sliced green onions
1 cup Arkansas basmati rice prepared according to package directions, and kept warm
Garnish: Chopped cilantro, toasted chopped pecans and slivered green onions

Cut chicken into 1-inch pieces and place in large bowl. Add Southern Comfort, soy sauce and cornstarch and mix well. Refrigerate for ½ hour.

Heat 2 tablespoons of vegetable oil in a large nonstick skillet over high heat.

When the pan is hot, add the marinated chicken pieces and stir-fry until golden brown and cooked through.

Pour in the Red Pepper Jelly Sauce and bring to a simmer. Cook until thickened, about 1 minute. Remove from heat and keep warm.

For the Green Tomato Fried Rice: Dice bacon and cook in a 12-inch cast iron skillet over medium high heat until crisp. Remove the bacon and drain on paper towels. Pour out all but 1 tablespoon of bacon grease. Return the cast iron skillet to medium high heat. Add green tomatoes, cooked bacon and green onions and sauté for one minute. Add the cooked rice and fold together. Cook briefly until all ingredients have heated through.

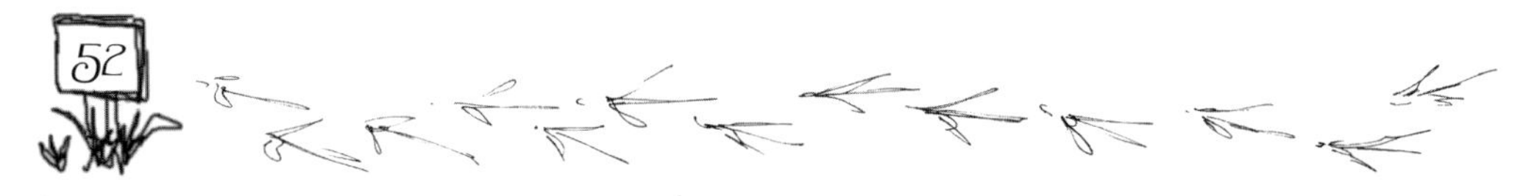

Portion rice onto four serving plates. Divide chicken and glaze evenly over each plate of rice.

Garnish with chopped cilantro, toasted pecans and slivered green onions.

Serves 4 - 6

Well I Declare!

Green tomatoes are only good fried in cornmeal. Don't you believe it! In this recipe, they provide a nice tang to balance the sweetness of the sauce.

Red Pepper Jelly Sauce

1/3 cup red pepper jelly
1 cup orange juice (freshly squeezed)
2 tablespoons rice wine vinegar
2 tablespoons hoisin sauce
2 teaspoons cornstarch
½ teaspoon salt
1 teaspoon Sriracha chili sauce
½ teaspoon sesame oil

Heat red pepper jelly in microwaveable bowl for 1 minute on 60% power. Whisk thoroughly and cool to room temperature.

Whisk in remaining ingredients and set aside until ready for use.

Yield: 1¼ cups

Cook's Secret:

Green pepper jelly is more common but it's well worth the extra effort to find the red which is available in both regular and hot. General Lee calls for the regular which provides just a bit of heat. Turn the heat up or down by adjusting the amount of the Sriracha chili sauce—where the real heat comes from.

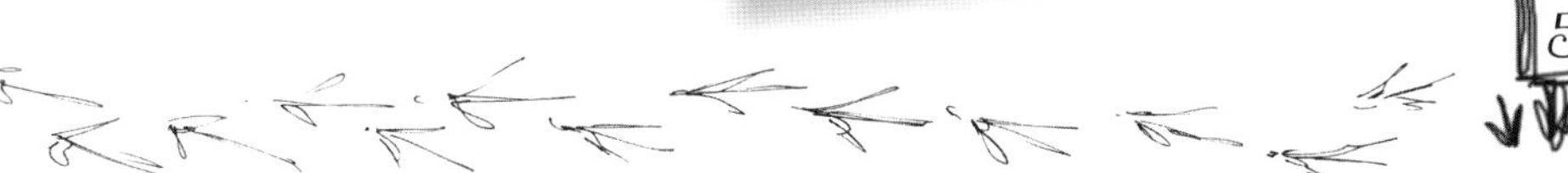

Gulf Coast Bake

This special occasion family recipe doesn't have to be for special occasions anymore—the ready availability of shrimp makes it possible to serve this dish any day of the week.

2 pounds chicken thighs, skin and excess fat removed
½ cup flour
2 teaspoons Creole seasoning
¼ cup canola oil
2 cups diced onion
1 cup diced celery
1 large green bell pepper, cut in thin strips
8 ounces sliced button mushrooms
1 teaspoon minced garlic
2 teaspoons minced fresh thyme
¼ teaspoon cayenne pepper
½ teaspoon salt
1 (14-ounce) can whole tomatoes, crushed by hand
1 cup dry white wine
2 tablespoons tomato paste
1 bay leaf
8 ounces cooked frozen cocktail shrimp, thawed
Steamed rice

Cook's Secret:

Using whole tomatoes, crushed by hand, allows the tomatoes to blend into the recipe better for a smoother texture and richer flavor.

Mix flour and Creole seasoning in a shallow bowl and set aside.

Heat oil over medium-high heat in a large sauté pan. Dredge the chicken in the seasoned flour and fry until golden brown, about 3 –4 minutes per side. Remove from the oil and drain on paper towels, then place in a casserole dish.

Discard all but one tablespoon of the oil and return the pan to the heat. Stir in the onion, celery, bell pepper, mushrooms, garlic, thyme, cayenne pepper and salt and sauté until the vegetables are crisp tender, about 4 minutes. Stir in the tomatoes, wine, tomato paste and the bay leaf and bring to a boil, then pour over the chicken in the casserole.

Cover and bake at 350° F for 40 minutes. Add the shrimp, pushing them down into the liquid, replace the cover and bake for another 5 minutes.

Serve over steamed rice. Serves 4

Scarlet Rice with Chicken

The addition of chicken and sausage transforms this traditional Low Country side dish into a one-pot entrée.

4 slices hickory or applewood smoked bacon, diced
¼ cup diced green pepper
½ cup diced sweet onion
¼ teaspoon coarse ground black pepper
¼ teaspoon cayenne pepper (optional)
8 ounces cooked smoked sausage, sliced lengthwise, then into ¼-inch slices
1 cup raw long grain white rice
1 (14½-ounce) can Italian seasoned diced tomatoes
½ cup tomato sauce
2 cups homemade or low-sodium chicken broth
1 cup diced poached chicken thighs (see recipe)
Garnish: Reserved cooked bacon

Fry bacon in a 12-inch sauté pan over medium-high heat until crisp. Remove the bacon and drain on paper towels. Pour off all but 2 tablespoons of bacon grease, then return the pan to medium-high heat. Add the green pepper, sweet onion, black pepper, cayenne pepper (if using) and sausage and sauté for about 2 – 3 minutes, until the sausage begins to brown and the vegetables begin to soften.

Add the rice, stirring well to coat it with the bacon grease, then pour in the diced tomatoes, tomato sauce, chicken broth and diced chicken. Bring the mixture to a boil, then reduce the heat to medium-low.

Cover tightly and simmer for 25 – 30 minutes or until rice is tender, stirring occasionally. Remove the pan from the heat and allow the rice to sit and steam for 5 minutes. Taste and adjust seasoning with salt and pepper. Serve immediately, garnished with reserved cooked bacon.

Serves 4

Well, I Declare!

Rice has been grown in the American South since the 17th Century and has just as long been a staple in Southern cuisine.

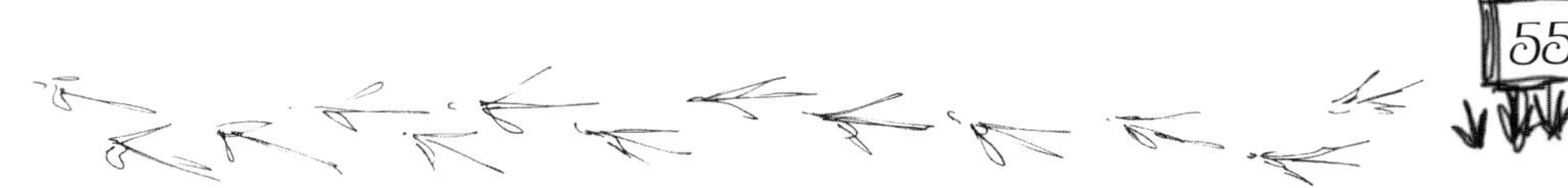

Sunshine State Stir-Fry

Every year when my family traveled to Florida, we stopped at the welcome center for a free (and welcomed) glass of fresh Florida orange juice. This recipe is inspired by those memories. Be sure to use fresh-squeezed juice or, at least, carton juice that is not from concentrate. Note: This is a variation on Sweet & Sour Chicken.

1½ pounds boneless, skinless chicken thighs

For the marinade:

2 tablespoons rice wine or sake
1½ tablespoons soy sauce
1 teaspoon sesame oil
½ teaspoon salt
1 teaspoon cornstarch

For the orange sauce:

1 cup fresh Florida orange juice
¼ cup plum sauce
3 tablespoons rice vinegar (unseasoned)
½ teaspoon sesame oil
¼ cup sugar
2 teaspoons cornstarch
½ teaspoon salt
½ teaspoon Sriracha chili sauce (Koon Chun brand)
4 tablespoons peanut oil, divided
½ teaspoon minced garlic
1 tablespoon minced fresh ginger
2 carrots, sliced thinly on the diagonal
1 (8-ounce) can sliced water chestnuts, drained and rinsed
1 (11-ounce) can mandarin oranges, drained
Steamed basmati or jasmine rice
Sliced scallions, for garnish

For the marinade: Trim chicken thighs of excess fat and cut into ½-inch pieces. Blend marinade ingredients in a small bowl and pour over chicken pieces. Mix well and allow to marinate at room temperature for ½ hour.

For the orange sauce: While the chicken is marinating, prepare the sauce. Whisk all sauce ingredients together in a small bowl and set aside.

Heat wok or large sauté pan over high heat. Add 3 tablespoons of peanut oil and swirl to coat the pan, then add the marinated chicken. Stir-fry quickly, until chicken turns brown, 2½ - 3 minutes. Remove the chicken from the pan and reserve. Drain off and discard the excess oil.

Wipe out the pan and return it to the heat. Add remaining tablespoon of oil and swirl to coat the pan. Add the garlic, ginger and carrots and stir-fry quickly for about 1 minute. Pour in the sauce and bring the mixture to a boil. Add the chicken and water chestnuts and cook for another minute. Remove from the heat and fold in the mandarin oranges.

Serve over steamed rice and garnish with sliced scallions.

Serves 4

Cook's Secret:

A note about some ingredients! The Sriracha Chili Sauce (Koon Chun brand) and a good plum sauce can be found in many grocery stores but certainly in any good Asian market. Both are worth the trip if you have to seek out an Asian market—and once there, you'll likely discover other exciting ingredients.

Maryland Fried Chicken

The Old Bay Seasoning gives this distinctive fried chicken that Eastern shore aroma and taste. Find it in the spice section of your grocery store or at the seafood counter. Remember to allow at least four hours for the chicken to marinate before frying.

8 chicken thighs (about 3½ - 4 pounds), trimmed of excess fat and skin

For the marinade:

2 cups buttermilk
1 tablespoon Old Bay Seasoning
1 tablespoon Louisiana-style hot sauce

For the breading:

1 cup flour
2 tablespoons cornstarch
2 tablespoons Old Bay Seasoning
1 tablespoon paprika
Vegetable oil for frying

For the marinade: Place the chicken thighs in a large bowl along with marinade ingredients. Mix well, then cover and refrigerate for at least 4 hours. Drain in a colander and discard the buttermilk mixture.

For the breading: Whisk the breading ingredients together in a shallow bowl or pie plate. Preheat the oven to 350° F.

Heat ½ inch of vegetable oil in a heavy aluminum or cast iron skillet over medium-high heat—a pinch of flour sprinkled in the oil should sizzle. Dredge the chicken in the seasoned flour and place in the hot oil. You will have to do this in batches to avoid overcrowding the pan. Fry 3 –4 minutes per side until golden brown. Remove from the skillet, drain on paper towels and place on a baking sheet or broiler pan.

Bake for 25 – 30 minutes. To check for doneness, cut a small slit near the bone and look inside to make sure the meat is white and no red remains—the juices should run clear.

Serves 4

Cook's Secret:

Starting in the skillet and finishing in the oven is a restaurant technique that helps keep the chicken from being so greasy.

Braised Chicken Thighs on Bluegrass Summer Succotash

This one-pot dish is best served at the height of summer when vegetables are at their peak of freshness and flavor. Side with a salad and your favorite buttermilk biscuits and this supper is complete.

6 slices applewood smoked bacon
¼ cup flour
1 teaspoon Creole seasoning
8 bone-in chicken thighs (3½ - 4 pounds), skin and excess fat removed
2 tablespoons vegetable oil
1 cup homemade or low-sodium chicken broth
¼ cup bourbon, divided

For the succotash:
4 ears of white or sweet yellow corn
1 cup fresh green beans, cut in 2-inch lengths
1 cup fresh baby limas or other fresh butter beans
½ cup cream
1 tablespoon minced fresh basil
Garnish: 1 cup diced tomatoes and reserved bacon

Fry bacon in a 12-inch heavy skillet (not non-stick). Remove the bacon and drain on paper towels, then finely chop and set aside. Pour all of the bacon grease out of the pan.

Return the skillet to medium-high heat and add 2 tablespoons of oil. Dredge chicken thighs in flour mixed with Creole seasoning. Brown for about 2 minutes per side or until golden brown. Fry in batches until all thighs have been pan-seared. Remove thighs from the skillet, drain on paper towels and set aside

Pour out all of the oil. Return the pan to medium high heat. Deglaze with chicken broth, scraping the bottom as the broth heats. Stir in 2 tablespoons of the bourbon then add the thighs back into the skillet. Reduce the heat to medium-low, cover and cook for 35 minutes or until tender.

For the succotash: Bring a large pot of salted water to a boil. Add corn on the cob and cook for 2 minutes. Remove with tongs and set aside. Add green beans to the same pot and cook for 9 – 11 minutes or until crisp tender. Remove with a slotted spoon, rinse with cold water, drain and place in medium bowl. Add lima beans to the same pot and cook for 12 – 20 minutes until tender and creamy. Cooking time will vary with age, size and variety of butter bean. Drain, rinse and add to bowl along with green beans.

Cut corn from the cob and mix with cooked green and lima beans. Set aside.

When the chicken has finished cooking, remove the thighs from the sauce and keep warm. Whisk in the cream, the remaining 2 tablespoons of bourbon and the fresh basil, then add the cooked corn and beans. Bring to a simmer, then reduce heat and cook for about 2 minutes.

Divide the succotash among 4 shallow bowls. Place two chicken thighs in each bowl, then garnish with diced tomatoes and diced bacon.

Serves 4

Index

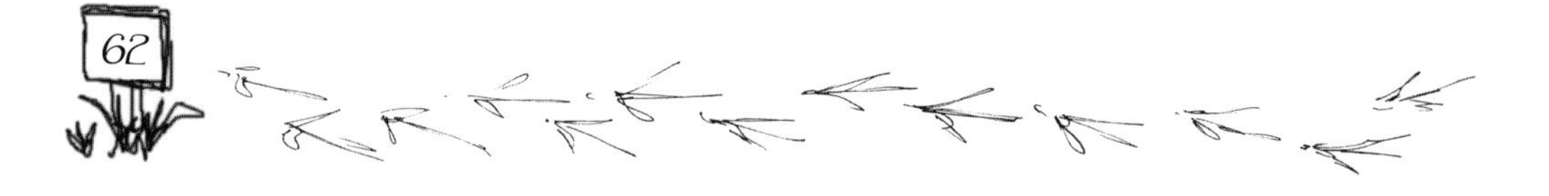

About the Cook

Sara Gibbs was born and raised in Western Maryland, just South of the Mason-Dixon Line. She holds a BS from West Virginia Wesleyan, an MLS from the University of Maryland, and a Culinary Arts Degree from Sullivan University. Her first career was as a public librarian and lasted fifteen years before her love of food and cooking asserted itself, leaving her no choice but to follow her heart and become a chef. Her love for the South and Southern food began in Maryland and grew throughout her life and travels, especially during summers on the North Carolina coast, winter vacations to Florida and, in recent years, annual trips to her husband's home state of Texas. Her recipes and food have appeared in national magazines and on local and national television. She is currently chef at Lynn's Paradise Café in Louisville, Kentucky. She lives a pastoral life with her husband, Tom, their two Quarter horses, Midget and Libby, and Shorty the Cat.